Attitude to the waqf property

Habibulla Yunuskhujayev

Attitude to the waqf property in Uzbekistan USSR in the XX century

LAP LAMBERT Academic Publishing RU

In this book one the Islamic custom – foundation and its traditions were mentioned. In addition to these, there stated the value of the foundation. Furthermore, it was analyzed motion, history and importance of it in the present time. However, at the beginning of the Russian colonial period, during the Soviet totalitarian system, at the time of the Soviet colonialism and the values associated with it, artificially destroyed, or even some of the values were destroyed.

One of such values is the Founding Institute, which was completed in 1928 in Uzbekistan. But it should be studied and studied as an integral part of our historical and cultural heritage and our past. Because statehood, education, social protection, prosperity, agriculture and the economic system were directly linked to the foundation property of the past. In historic sources and historical documents, we find documents and information about foundations and foundations.

As in the case of the falsification of the true history during the Soviet era and the devastation of the millennial traditions of our people, the concept of the foundation was very limited and unambiguous, and the concept of the foundation was introduced only in relation to the place of mosque and madrasahs. It is sad to say that even a great number of historian scholars only define the definition and the concept above. In fact, the concept of the foundation is a concept, value, or socio-spiritual institution that plays a very important role in our religious, spiritual and socio-economic life that needs to be interpreted in a broader sense.

The author express gratitude to Zafar Adilov for his scientific and practical assistance!

Author

CONTENTS

INTRODUCTION

In the last quarter of the 1920s, the Central Asian republics of the UUSR underwent a period of social, economic, and cultural turmoil which constituted the local form of the "cultural revolution" which Sheila Fitzpatrick described for Russia. Mobilization and repressive measures against what the Party labelled as "feudal-patriarchal relics" lay at the core of such "cultural revolution" in the Central Asian village. These measures focused on a struggle for the emancipation of women, generally known as attack. Their most powerful image was that of the unveiling of Central Asian women and the ritual burning of their discarded headgear. The attack was accompanied and immediately followed by virulent anti-religious initiatives, which targeted both religious institutions (schools, mosques, shrines, etc.) and those who were staffing them in various roles.

One component of this unprecedented attack against Islam in the region was the completion of the offensive against Islamic pious endowments (waqf), especially in the Uzbek USR. The proportion of waqf has been estimated at between one-tenth and one-fifth of total agricultural land (in the Bukharan emirate) at the end of the 19th century, which makes the issue of the destiny of these estates an intrinsically interesting one—not to mention the fact that Islamic institutions depended on endowments for their day-to-day functioning. The erosion of the economic basis of the production and transmission of Islamic formal knowledge, as well as of the maintenance of mosques and their staff, must be understood in the framework of a general move towards the modernization of Central Asia in its specific Soviet form. Both local Muslim intellectuals and the Bolsheviks shared a fascination for "modernization."

Their views on the matter, though, were diametrically opposed as far as the role of religion in society was concerned. While "anticlericalism" was not

4

the exclusive preserve of Communist atheist propaganda, Central Asian intellectuals — including those temporarily co-opted into the Soviet and Party systems — were wary of advocating the eradication of religion as such. The confrontation between these two tendencies marks the political and cultural history of early Soviet Central Asia, and has been studied for the last decade in comparison with the Middle and Near East, where "modernization" often equaled "secularization." Soviet policies towards waqf in Central Asia, too, can be regarded as a "secularization" measure: yet, their final goal was the erasure of religion, rather than its separation from the State and its containment in a distinct sphere.

This article discusses the destiny of those waqf holdings (in particular, of land plots in rural areas) which the Soviet administrative language classified as "religious" rather than "cultural" — by this, meaning that the income they generated was allotted not to schools, but to mosques, shrines, or hostels (khanaqas).

This distinction was not always clear, and may have reflected a simplistic administrative framework, rather than real differences; however, as this article will discuss, the opposition between "religious" and "cultural" waqf had historical roots and possessed, in the early Soviet years, a political rationale. The actors involved made sense of these notions, essentially because such a distinction existed in legally binding texts produced by the new Bolshevik regime: it would thus be impossible to write the history of waqf institutions in the early Soviet period without referring, however critically, to this "religious" vs. "cultural" dichotomy.

Religious waqf survived more or less unscathed through the land reforms of the 1920s, but in 1927 they came under direct attack on the basis of a written norm. This meant that, until 1927, a number of pious endowments survived. It is impossible to quantify the proportion of "cultural" vs. "religious" endowments, or to ascertain whether these labels were indeed appropriate: what matters here is that this distinction allowed the preservation of some waqf, and that in 1927 this ceased to be true. The fundamental historical problem of who unleashed this attack, and under which circumstances, is worth exploring as such: all the more so, as the answer to these questions is somewhat unexpected and helps to reshape our understanding of a variety of features of early Soviet rule in Central Asia — and possibly beyond.

In this article, I will focus on the origin of these legal provisions underlying the expropriation and nationalization of religious waqf. This is better done by following step-by-step the chronology of acts that led up to such legal provisions, and then by looking very closely at the drafting process from which the latter resulted. I demonstrate how the practical decision to seize religious waqf (more exactly, to nationalize the rural land plots that constituted their underlying capital) first coalesced locally, in the easternmost part of the Fergana province, only then to be embraced by Party and Soviet organs in Samarkand and Tashkent. While this does not mean that this locally-generated idea was forced upon republican and regional (i.e. Central Asian) organs, it does still mean that it was not a diktat from Moscow that led to the ultimate legal formalization of the expropriation of this residual category of Islamic endowments.

The interest of focusing on such a minute episode is threefold. First, this is a still unexplored phase in the story of Central Asian waqf from the revolution to their complete abolition. Hence, this article attempts to fill a gap in our empirical knowledge of what occurred to these institutions in the 1920s. As we will see more in detail elsewhere, these waqfs had been under attack in the early years of Soviet rule in Turkestan. Yet, a more conciliatory attitude prevailed in the period of the New Economic Policy, which was in

6

turn superseded by the advent of violent anti-religious campaigns from 1927. I must emphasize, however, that this article is rather a study in Soviet history, than an inquiry into waqf as an Islamic institution at the time. This is clearly reflected in the source base (documents stemming from Party and Soviet organs), as well as in the way I approach it. Yet, the reconstruction of when, where, how, and why the Soviet government of the Uzbek USR decided for the first time to nationalize religious waqf may prove useful to scholars who are interested in the internal life, juridical nature, and socio-economic function of pious endowments at the time.

Second, while the historiography of Soviet anti-religious policies has largely focused on their ideological aspects, intellectual background, and consequences (within the UUSR and in terms of their international resonance), less attention has been devoted to the decision-making process behind them, and even less to the latter's textual dimension. This is generally true for other domains in the history of the Soviet period, especially in the "peripheries." Decrees and resolution have a life after their publication, and sometimes they have an ideological or cultural "prehistory": yet their most recent past (the drafting process) is unexplored.

One is left with the feeling that anti-religious measures in Central Asia "were implemented," or "happened." It is often hard to discern the agency behind these policies, while the agency of those directly touched by them (for instance, Central Asian women in the case of hujum) has been, by comparison, quite extensively explored.This bottom-up approach has allowed historians and their readers a grasp of social history that would have been inconceivable if one had focused solely on Soviet and Party institutions. It is enough to compare Shoshana Keller's and Marianne Kamp's work to understand the difference between these two approaches: the first is our best guide to the deployment of Soviet anti-Islamic policies in

7

the region up to WWII, while the second epitomizes a new attention to culture and grass-roots social dynamics, on the basis of a largely different source base. The two approaches are more complementary than opposed, although the first seems to have become unfashionable in recent years. Yet, the complete rejection of "institutionalist" history risks making us forget that laws, decrees, and resolutions had a performative character, that is: they could (and, in principle, should) create the state of things they outlined. While it is heuristically productive to consider agency as diffuse throughout society, rather than concentrated in the Party or state systems, one should not forget that some of the players in this game could coerce the behavior of others by means of textual production: hence, the interest in who produced these texts, and how. Here I contrive to demonstrate the potential of a focus on chains of command and document-drafting at multiple levels, to produce a more precise view of how policies took shape. This effort not only adds texture to the narrative of the Soviet attack on religion: it also helps in clarifying issues of historical responsibility. In other words, I argue that decision-making (and, above all, writing) can be regarded as social processes worth studying as such, insofar as they serve as a diagnostic of power and its resources.

Third, and somewhat related, this exercise in the quasi-philological reconstruction of how this legislation came into being is revealing of the multi-centric nature of Soviet power (at least in these years and in this region) and of the need to re-consider the notion of "periphery" on the basis of how power relations actually worked on the ground—which might, or might not, coincide with the hierarchy of administrative units. In the decision to expropriate religious waqf, the political weight of a single province was decisive, the more "central" (regional and republican) agencies could subsume, but ultimately not restrain it. Possibly because of its population and its economic importance for the cultivation of cotton and the related industry, Andijan might have been in an exceptionally good position to play such a role, therefore positioning itself (at least subjectively) as a propulsive "center." It was not the first time, and it would not be the last, that this occurred in the Uzbek USR of the 1920s.

That Soviet power was not as monolithic as the old "totalitarian" school had assumed is now well ascertained, thanks to the work of "revisionist" historians. However, while these approaches have gone a long way in general Soviet history (and have even spurred a "post-revisionist" scholarship), the history of Soviet Central Asia has not yet fully benefitted from such shifts. As hinted at above, all the most recent historiography contains a strong attention to power dynamics "from below" and Soviet subjectivity: but such attention is somewhat limited in two directions. First, the prevailing influence of "post-colonial" and "subaltern" approaches means that the dominant paradigm remains focused on Soviet experiments in social engineering (whether successful or unsuccessful is immaterial here) and, conversely, dynamics of resistance, rather than highlighting the participation of local actors in the dialectical formulation of the Soviet power framework.

Second, in cases where such a participation has been emphasized, this has almost exclusively been done in relation to the definition of boundaries or nationality policies: much less has been written about the way the agency of local Party workers shaped Soviet agrarian policies, rather than simply opposing resistance to it. While we are now ready to accept that Central Asians at the lower levels of the Party and Soviet pyramids (or even out of them) were able and willing to navigate and appropriate the system in matters of nationality and culture, in other fields (e.g. economic policies) the "subjection" of these actors still hits the eye more vividly than their "subjectivity." In particular, historiography has not yet gauged and explained the eagerness of some to join the system, reap the fruits of ideological credibility and political loyalty, and hope for rewards in the form of investments or public expenditure. To focus on consensus does not mean to deny the violence, resistance, and repression, which formed an integral part of Soviet rule at the time. Yet, the picture would not be complete if we did not include the set of practical incentives, political opportunities, and ideological appeal on which Bolshevik power on the spot was relying with success. All these circumstances can be explored at the republican as well as at the provincial (okrug) level: it is this second key that this article employs.

The villages for which the expropriation of religious waqf was first decreed were the object of a border modification in 1927. They belonged to the canton of Aim (in Uzbek, Oim; Aimskaia volost' in Russian), which had been assigned to the Kara-Kirgiz Autonomous Province (KKAO in acronym) on the occasion of the "national delimitation" (razmezhevanie) of 1924. The story of the delimitation in general has been thoroughly explored, as well as the subsequent alterations of inter-republican borders. Historians from independent Kyrgyzstan, in particular, have argued that these revisions resulted from a "special treatment" of Uzbek claims, if compared to the requests of the Kyrgyz component of the population of the localities in question. Western students of this question have rather emphasized the appropriation of the Soviet "national" discourse by the actors involved, as well as the importance of economic policy measures that were being implemented at the same time, namely the land-and-water reform.

This article explains how these two circumstances — the revision of the border in Aim and the need for those six rural communities to "catch up" with the new framework for land rights that already existed in the Uzbek UUSR — created opportunities for the local communist clique, based in

10

Andijan, to position itself as the spearhead of the new line of the Party towards Islam and other "patriarchal relics." By emphasizing the relevance of local power dynamics and by looking at the attack campaign and at the sovietization of land rights in Aim as parallel phenomena, rather than in isolation, this article shows how the land reform decree for Aim became a terrain of confrontation between those who wanted to accelerate the attack on Islamic institutions, and those who advocated a more prudent policy. In this, the paper pins down the chronology, geographic spread, and modality of the attack on waqf, while also helping to nuance our views on the origins and enactment of Soviet anti-Islamic policies by questioning "top-down" narratives.

BACKGROUND: PRESSURE ON WAQF
UP TO THE LAND REFORM

While the task of writing a history of waqf property in early Soviet Uzbekistan is best left to specialists with direct access to the relevant documents, here it is useful to summarize how Bolshevik policy towards waqf land in Central Asia evolved throughout the first post-revolutionary decade, as this is essential to appreciate what happened in Aim. The first Bolshevik attack on waqf of all kinds, linked to the tentative enactment of wholesale land nationalization mentioned above, was indeed short-lived: as related by Pianciola and Sartori, until 1922 "Turkestan Bolsheviks' attitude towards waqf was ambiguous," and, besides the appointment of sympathetic mutawallis, and decisions pertaining to which people's commissariat should administer waqf income "can only help us to understand the intentions of the Russian Bolsheviks of

Turkestan," the implementation of such measures remaining very superficial. Partly because they were confronted with serious concerns of public order and armed opposition both inside and outside Turkestan, the new Soviet regime decided to normalize its relations with local Muslims and their institutions. Yet, it was in August 1921 that the 6th Turkestan Party congress established the distinction between "cultural" and "religious" waqf, which would constitute the conceptual basis for subsequent policies. Such an appeasement would be completed in June 1922, with the "restitution of waqfs to madrasas and mosques."

At the very end of December 1922, a decree of the Turkestan central executive committee established the Main Waqf Administration (Glavnoe vakufnoe upravlenie, or GVU). This office, included in the people's commissariat for education (Narkompros), was responsible for the management of the revenues from cultural and educational waqfs. As these

12

pious foundations served to finance maktabs and madrasas, this could be interpreted as a token of reconciliation with the Turkestani intelligentsia which populated the commissariat for education and fostered its own agenda of educational reform under the (temporary) aegis of the new regime. Yet, the decree itself resulted from the desire to exclude another organization from the management of waqf income, which was equally interested in exerting its influence on the schooling system, namely the mahkama-i shari'a (shari'a boards) at the district level. The transfer of authority to the GVU did not take place without the fierce opposition of this organization, while the local documents from Andijan which Sartori used vividly depict the confusion that reigned in 1922-1923, including the incomplete transfer to the GVU of previously "municipalized" waqf property.

It took almost three years to complete the catalogue of all waqf property in the Uzbek USR, with the exception of some newly constituted endowments. The degree of knowledge (or, indeed, ignorance) the Soviet government and, before, the Russian colonial authorities, had of waqf in Turkestan is controversial. The impression one derives from the extant literature on the multiple efforts to collect, classify, and apprehend the economic nature of Islamic pious endowments since the late 1860s is one of an endless series of administrative drills, the efficacy of each remaining dubious, and the knowledge they produced destined to rapid obsolescence. While each of these drills was meant as a step towards the legibility of waqf, it is doubtful that such goal would be attained before waqf itself came under threat. This partly derived from an inconsistency in the practical aims of such legibility: while in the Tsarist period the focus seems to have been on the fiscal position of endowments, especially after the first edition of the Turkestan Statute in 1886, in the early Soviet period a growing ambition to grapple and regulate these institutions' property took shape. This bears similarities to the shift from Tsarist to Soviet policies towards land in general in the mid-1920s, as exemplified in the titling ("land registration") that took place on the occasion of the land-and-water reform of 1925-1926, on which I will comment below.

A specific problem within the general question of the legibility of waqf concerns the distinction between "religious" and "cultural" waqf. In theory, it was simple: income from "religious" waqf benefitted a mosque, or a shrine, or a hostel; that from "cultural" waqf benefitted a school, either elementary (mak- tab) or advanced (madrasa). In practice, things were more complex: as noted by Sartori and others, it was not uncommon to be confronted with "mixed" endowments, where a variety of real estate (e.g. rural land, caravanserais, bazaar stalls...) generated income for multiple beneficiary institutions, both "religious" and "cultural." Not only that; the Tsarist administration was already aware of the fact that in many cases part of the income flowed into the pockets of the endower's descendants, from whom religious staff (i.e. muezzins, teachers, imams...) and, more importantly, the administrator (mutawalli) were chosen. Tsarist officers had indeed set up the category of "private waqf" (chast- nyi vakuf) to designate these cases, but soon realized that this term applied to the share of the income which was "privately" appropriated, rather than to a distinct typology of waqf. The most important distinction that Tsarist legislation made, though, was not between "religious" and "cultural" endowments, but instead between the endowment of "populated" and "unpopulated" land: this distinction existed for fiscal purposes and in order to "fit" waqf land in the general framework of colonial land surveying. The distinction between "religious" and "cultural," thus, did not exist before the 6th Turkestan Party congress in 1921, as noted above.

If it is hard to find a precedent in Tsarist regulations for the distinction between "religious" and "cultural" waqf, one can nonetheless argue that pre-revolutionary practices had introduced two important precedents to early Soviet rules. First, Tsarist regulations supposed that the income generated by waqf estates could be split more or less accurately between different beneficiaries—"private" or institutional.

On paper at least, if one could distinguish between what was benefitting a mosque and what was benefitting the mutawalli, why couldn't one distinguish between the income destined to a mosque and, for instance, a school? Thus in a way, State organs had already begun meddling (or aspiring to meddle) with the internal allocation of waqf income even before 1921. Second, article 299 of the Turkestan Statute had decreed that, in the case of "populated" waqf land, the Treasury should pay back the land tax, fully or pro-quota, to the beneficiary institutions, if the land had been recognized as exempted from taxation.

This meant that before 1917 some bureaucratic infrastructure already existed for returning to schools and mosques that part of the rent which the colonial State had appropriated in the form of land tax. If this allocation of the tax part of the rent had been conceivable before 1917, why couldn't it be extended to the whole of the rent this "populated" land generated? One could even venture to argue that it was the mechanism of article 299 of the Turkestan Statute, together with the knowledge basis it supposed, that allowed the ambitious post-revolutionary project of distinguishing between "religious" and "cultural" waqf. Indeed, we know for certain that Soviet land statistics in the mid-1920s relied on the lists of waqf holdings which the colonial land-tax assessment commissions had compiled for the Andijan uezd: both the former and the latter included a census of waqf, which associated each plot with the institution it benefitted.

If this explains how the distinction between "religious" and "cultural" waqf could be implemented, it does not explain how it became prominent. This is a particularly interesting question, as such a distinction was not commonplace in the Muslim "peripheries" of the UUSR where waqf existed. The answer belongs to the domain of intellectual history and would require a separate study. However, it is still worth highlighting a few circumstances. First, the idea that the State could centralize the management of waqf revenues (ideally, to reduce abuses and to pool resources in the most effective way) was neither new nor Bolshevik: it had been implemented for almost a century prior to this in the Ottoman empire.

In Central Asia the idea that funding for improved native schools could be derived from waqf which had been transferred to Russian colonial institutions had first been considered in the 1880s under the Turkestan governor-general Mikhail G. Cherniaev, but to no avail. Possibly because of the circulation of ideas between Istanbul and Bukhara, or with an eye to more recent discussions in Turkestan, the 1917 reform program of the Young Bukharans conjured the establishment of a new "special body" for the administration of "those [waqf] destined for Bukhara's national education." "If the revenues deriving from these were straightened out and if the expenditure were used properly"—enthusiastically continued the program—"Bukhara could in the domain of education surpass the most developed city in Europe." Second, the emphasis on the "deserving poor" in need of education was one of the terrains on which some (ambiguous) agreement could be reached, after the revolution, between the same intellectuals and Bolshevik power: in 1919, a preference existed, within the Soviet government of Turkestan, for "public" waqf, which were meant "to give material and spiritual help" to those who did not have sufficient means to receive education. In other words, as a first approximation, one could argue that a special consideration for "cultural" waqf was already embedded in the way the idea of a "separate exchequer," or directorate for pious endowments had been welcomed and adapted in Bukhara. In addition, such "decoupling" between the two categories went down well in the context of the confrontation and ever-uncertain alliance of Russian Bolsheviks and Muslim "reformist" politicians.

To sum up, by the middle of the 1920s all waqf properties were meant to be administered by the GVU and its branches, in principle with the exception of rural populated land, which should have been nationalized. In practice, however, a report on the situation in August 1925 explained that such nationalization had not taken place, and that the GVU limited itself to supervising the rights of those who tilled that land. The decree of December 1922 and subsequent specifications had virtually confirmed the land rights of those peasants, but in practice the latter kept on paying a rent. The only difference for them, was that now the money was meant to be channeled to a school through the local GVU office (which could pool resources), rather than through a mutawalli, and that there was some control over the amount they were conferring. From another viewpoint, if compared to the Tsarist period, now a State organ had at its disposal the entirety of the rent that the waqf was generating: before, according to art. 299 of the Turkestan Statute, the Treasury could simply reimburse the tax that had been paid out of such rent despite the notarized text of the foundation.

The situation was further complicated by the involvement of the organs of local economic governance, or mestkhozy, a category that included the Municipal Economic Administration: first, because some of these organs had retained their control over waqf holdings and their management, after the incomplete "demunicipalization" of 1922-23; second, because in 1925 the GVU was encouraged to rent out to the mestkhozy some of the waqf holdings that had passed under GVU management. In this case, the mestkhozy themselves would take on the role of managing the resulting income, with the proviso that 28 per cent of the revenues would serve educational needs, especially for women. Finally, should previously concealed waqf holdings be discovered after Summer 1925, they would be transferred to the mestkhozy.[39] Indeed, evidence collected by Keller suggests that, in 1925, local GVU branches were struggling with the mestkhozy for control over pious endowments and their income, in the context of systematic lack of liquidity for all sorts of economic activity, both licit and illicit. As a result, even in the second half of 1925 the regulation of waqf properties was still unclear, due to the stratification of several measures, each of them having received a different degree of practical enactment.

THE LAND-AND-WATER REFORM AND "CULTURAL" WAQF

Pianciola and Sartori write that the land-and-water reform decreed in 1925 in the Uzbek USR "was the first step towards the abolition of waqf, which came at the end of the 1920s in all Central Asian republics." They correctly noted that, on the occasion of such a reform, the acquisition of waqf land by the State land fund was limited to cultural waqf and left religious waqf untouched. Here I will explore the specificities of this process, by emphasizing the geography of the attack on cultural waqf in different provinces of the Uzbek USR. I will also highlight the contradictions between different pieces of legislation concerning waqf at the same time (late 1925), and, consequently, the substantial ambiguity and hesitations that characterized the practical attitude of the Soviet government at this stage.

In December 1925 and in the first months of 1926, a "first wave" of land-and-water reform, based on a specific decree, took place in the three "core provinces" (korennye oblasti) of the Uzbek USR, namely those of Tashkent, Fergana, and Samarkand. The term "core" refers here to the fact that the territory of these provinces had been part of Russian Turkestan, rather than of one of the protectorates. A stronger (though by no means wholly satisfactory) grasp on the territory and population, the repression of the basmachi uprising, basic Soviet institution-building and, above all, the presence of Tsarist land assessment data made attempts at the transformation of agrarian relations and land rights in these provinces more likely to succeed than in the former People's Republics of Bukhara and Khiva.

The Zeravshan province, where Bukhara itself was located, was the object of a thorough statistical survey in 1926 and of a "second wave" of reform in the winter between 1926 and 1927 — hence, one year later than in the "core provinces." I will mention again the decree of the land- and-water

19

reform in Zeravshan. Here, it is enough to note that the complete requisition of land and agricultural implements (including draught animals) did concern not only large and absentee landowners, merchants and craftsmen (above a certain benchmark), and, as we know, cultural waqf: it also affected the properties of "former emiral dignitaries," including Islamic judges and muftis. This objectively resulted in an attack on the "clergy," although its goal was getting rid of any of those who had colluded with the regime of the former emir.

However, neither the first, nor this second wave of reform concerned the Aim canton because, as we know, it still belonged in its entirety to Kirgizia (which in 1926 changed its name and status: from the Kara-Kirgiz Autonomous province to the Kara-Kirgiz Autonomous UUSR). This was one reason why, in 1927, after the six allegedly Uzbek rural communities of the canton had been assigned to the Uzbek USR, local Party and Soviet leaders, mostly in Andijan, decided that the six village communities had to "catch up" with the rest of Fergana and undergo the land reform — if possible, in an improved form relative to what had happened elsewhere. The second, implicit reason for such a hurry was that the reform in Aim was a chance for them to shine in the eyes of their neighbors and bosses. As we will see in the next section, this had a direct connection with the attitude of the Andijani communists towards religious waqfs.

Moreover, we should bear in mind that neither the decree for Fergana, Tashkent, and Samarkand, nor the one for Zeravshan ordered the complete expropriation of Islamic pious endowments (waqf): on the contrary, only properties endowed as "educational" waqf were confiscated in the framework of the first two waves of land reform, while the decrees did not mention the destiny of those that belonged to religious ones. In this respect, the land-and-water reform of 1925-1926 did not immediately alter much the juridical and administrative framework in which waqf had survived so far, as we have summarized it in the previous section, on the basis of the existing literature.

The decree on the reform in the provinces of Fergana, Tashkent, and Samarkand of 2 December 1925 was quite linear. In the case of waqf property, it established that all educational and cultural waqf land was transferred to the People's Commissariat for agriculture (Narkomzem), to be included in the "State land stock" available for redistribution. This decision—in particular the exclusion of religious waqf from the scope of the reform—had emerged after much discussion throughout the Spring and Summer of 1925, when some religious waqf land had been the object of seizures in Fergana: for instance, intervening in Andijan in May, at a time when republican Party organs were interested in containing a soaring wave of land-squatting, the people's commissar for agriculture of the Uzbek USR, Abdurahim Khojibaev, ordered the end of the seizure of religious waqf land and even stated that the imams of the mosques concerned should be exempted from the land-tax as a form of compensation.

This corresponded to the official position on this matter which Ak- mal Ikramov had enunciated in March. As reported by Keller, in June 1925, the executive bureau of the Uzbek Party manifested the intention to strengthen and expand the authority of the GVU, but expressed caution in dealing with religious waqf.[45] The question of the destiny of "mosques' own waqf" was raised again, but not answered at all, at the SredAzBiuro plenum of July 1925. An ex post account of the events suggests that a proposal to confiscate the land of religious waqf that exceeded a given standard (norma) was formulated again in Andijan in August 1925, but had not been endorsed before the publication of the land reform decree of December 1925. All in all, although some sources seem to suggest that some "large" waqf were

21

confiscated before the land reform had started, it is unclear whether these comprised religious waqf—and even if the religious waqf had been seized and redistributed in the spring and summer of 1925, available evidence seems to suggest that this was happening without any strong endorsement on the part of the republican Party and Soviet organs of the UzUSR.

Certainly the reform did not concern religious waqf, and even after the reform they were still firmly in place, as subsequent vicissitudes demonstrate. Keller was right when she noted that, on 19 December 1925 (i.e. two weeks after the decree of the land reform), the central executive committee of the Uzbek USR passed a bill "on waqf." According to this bill the only waqf that were not transferred to the Narkomzem were those "located beyond the city boundaries and occupied by vineyards and gardens": the inclusion in the land stock available for redistribution, thus, should have included the bulk of religious waqf on agricultural land. The bill itself, however, was not immune from internal inconsistency, as a previous article stated that "waqf properties owned by religious societies" would be the object of "a special legislative act." Neither Keller nor I, has managed to pin down this special law on religious waqf. While it is unclear what happened to the educational waqf which had already been transferred to the mestkhozy, both the 19 December bill and common sense suggest that they were not transferred to the Narkomzem but remained at the disposition of these local organs.

In other words, in December 1925 two contradictory regulations saw the light: the decree on the land reform, which excluded religious waqf from its scope, and then the bill "on waqf," which in an ambiguous manner ordered their nationalization and transfer to the Narkomzem. In all likelihood, it was the decree on the land reform that prevailed: for the moment, religious waqf were largely spared. According to Keller, already on 30 December 1925 an

22

amendment allowed the retention of religious waqf on woodland and orchards. Almost one year after the reform, many religious waqf were still in place, for instance in the Khojent district of the Samarkand province (where "up to 88% of all waqf property belong[ed] to the clergy") and in the Fergana province. In the latter a variety of waqf goods that should have been confiscated according to the bill of 19 December 1925 resisted through 1926: not only apricot orchards, but also "other mosque lands," and even non-land waqf goods (mills, stalls) which provided income to religious institutions. In short, "income from religious waqf ... remain[ed] almost entirely in the hands of the clergy." Between the land reform decree and the bill "on waqf," the former had prevailed, at least in that it safeguarded the interest of endowments which provided funding for mosques. And yet, the contrast between the two norms passed in December 1925 reflects the hesitation and contortionism that surrounded decision-making on religious waqf. We will find the same contortionism and embarrassment in the case of the land reform in Aim.

All this meant that, after the land reform in Fergana there remained, broadly speaking, two types of waqf: on the one hand, as we saw in the last two paragraphs, the religious waqf, which financed a mosque or a khanaqa (pilgrim guesthouse, usually associated to a shrine or a sufi order or a particular ishan), that is: all the waqfs which did not support a school (or other educational institutions); on the other, waqfs that supported a school, but were constituted by the endowment of goods other than land — quite typically, bazaar stalls, but also mills and bathhouses. In addition, at the local level many were aware that educational waqfs still existed, and that their land had not been confiscated and redistributed with the 1925-1926 land reform. The land reform, by transferring the land of "cultural" waqf to the Narkomzem, significantly curtailed the funding available for Islamic

23

schools. It also greatly simplified the situation, by reducing the typology of existing pious endowments: on the eve of the reform "cultural" waqf were, as we know, sometimes managed by the GVU of the Narkompros, sometimes by the mestkhozy, and sometimes their administration was outsourced by the former to the latter. This simplification had its appeal, which might in turn explain why the 1925 reform decree prevailed over the enactment of the other concurrent bill of 19 December 1925.

CHANGING ATTITUDES

In 1927, the Uzbek USR underwent a process of internal administrative delimitation known as raionirovanie. As the word suggests, this consisted in abolishing the intermediate uezd level inherited from the Tsarist period, in re-grouping the cantons (volosti) in districts (raiony), loosely defined on the basis of economic similarities, and in setting up okrugi as territorial units bigger than the uezdy but smaller than the old provinces (oblasti), which consequently disappeared.

The raionirovanie reshuffled the organization of the GVU, by establishing two kinds of local institutions for their governance, namely city-level and rayon-level "Waqf departments" (vakufnye otdely). It appears that the rayon departments were not properly equipped for such a role: for instance, they either neglected their duties, or they were simply unable to keep their accounting books in order. This made the need for a further simplification in the categorization of waqf properties even more desirable, independently from political considerations about the relation between Soviet power and Islamic institutions.

Such a noticeable turn in the Soviet attitude towards religion and, by consequence, towards Islamic schools and pious endowments, took place in 1927. Historiography has described how, in that year, the symbolic date of March 8 served to unleash an unprecedented attack on the specific "patriarchal relics" embodied in the veil and in the seclusion of women. This was part of a more general offensive against

Islamic practice and institutions, including schools, which were also suffering from the competing creation of Soviet educational institutions. As an Andijan communist would describe it with hindsight, such an offensive against the Islamic schools in 1927-1928 consisted in a mixture of propaganda and administrative measures to "asphyxiate" them: schools lost students because they could only have pupils above the age of 14 and, in the case of old-method schools, could not teach "Soviet sciences"; they also lost funding, because of new rules concerning waqf properties.

Hence, it was not by chance that less than a week after the fateful 8 March 1927, a meeting of the executive bureau of the Uzbek communist Party discussed the future of waqf estates, and did so in an apparently unemotional and non-ideological manner, so far as the minutes tell us. The bureau started out by endorsing once again the distinction between educational and religious waqfs, and by recognizing that the former were now State property, and their income was administered by the Narkompros for educational needs.

However, it went on stating that, for practical reasons, if would have been better if the Narkompros (i.e. the GVU and its branches) handed over the exploitation of the endowed estates to the local or, municipal mestkhozy, on the basis of ad hoc contracts. This meant that the Party was finally taking sides in the struggle between mestkhozy and GVU branches which had started at least two years before—and it was doing so in a way that, objectively if not self-consciously, ended up syphoning off the income from non-land "cultural" waqf which the GVU was still controlling.

True, all the income would still be re-directed to the Narkompros: but the introduction of a layer between it and the waqfs themselves would have reduced the scope for interventions by the Narkompros, and weakened the institutional link between the waqf itself and the school it pertained to. In March 1927 the Uzbek communist Party did not yet venture to comment on the status of religious waqfs. This was an issue which the executive bureau explicitly put off, by relating it to the discussion and solution of the question of the "Muslim clergy" as a whole. Uzbek republican Party authorities would re-consider this issue again in June.

The Central Asian Bureau considered the issue of the "clergy" in its 13th Plenum at the end of May 1927 in the context of the hujum campaign. More specifically, though, the Bureau had received alarmed messages from the Uzbek Party authorities about the growing influence of the Spiritual Administration, and in particular of the mahkamai shari'a in Andijan, by means of the appointment of the directors of new-method schools from among its supporters. As a result, by the end of May 1927, the Uzbek executive bureau abandoned its March reticence and openly stated that "reformed" Islamic schools should be withdrawn from the sphere of influence of the Spiritual Administration, rather than trying to "starve" them by transferring waqf income to the mestkhozy.

In its examination of the question, the Central Asian Bureau considered the current Soviet attitude towards the "Muslim clergy" in Central Asia as inadequate and probably obnoxious: the time had ended — it wrote — when one could think about using the cleavages within such "clergy" and forge an alliance with its most "enlightened," reformist segments. From now on, the "clergy" should be regarded as a "united reactionary mass," "an indivisible component of the field which is hostile to us." Its internal cleavages were not real, but only "the expression of the struggle between different social groupings (gruppirovki)." The Soviet regime had tolerated the social and economic role of the Islamic "clergy": now some prominent religious leaders, such as Turakhan Makhdum, in Kokand and elsewhere, were profiting from this situation, to the point of portraying themselves in the vernacular press as indispensable intermediaries between Soviet power and the masses. The "clergy" exerted its influence in particular through the school system (especially through "reformed" schools), which functioned as a channel to reach, beyond the children, their families, so that the "clergy" explained to them "how to use the Soviet legislation."

To remedy this situation, the Bureau recommended grappling with the issue of all waqf holdings: "the alienation in favor of the State" of cultural-educational waqfs (as on the occasion of the land reform of 1925-1926) was considered insufficient. One needed to expropriate all pious endowments, including those supporting mosques, and to transfer the management of their income "to local peasant committees of mutual help." The subtext here was that all pious endowments should be subtracted from the control of the GVU of the Narkom- pros, and be transferred to other agencies.

This shift was needed to contain the influence of the Central Spiritual Administration (dukhovnoe upravlenie) and its local branches, which allegedly maintained strong ties with the local branches of the GVU itself. Hence at the end of May 1927 the idea of the expropriation of "religious" waqf found some support in the Plenum of the Central Asian Bureau of the Party, which was meeting in Tashkent. This idea was linked to the Party line towards the "Muslim clergy," rather than to its land policy. Furthermore, it did not imply the redistribution of the endowed land estates, but only the transfer of the rent that flowed from them from Islamic institutions to "peasant committees."

The decisions of the 13th Plenum of the Central Asian Bureau on religious waqf needed to be translated into practical measures. The way this was done is quite enlightening. According to Keller, in June 1927 first the executive bureau and then (June 14) the Plenum of the central committee of the Uzbek Communist Party approved the expropriation of religious waqf, "although at this point there were no clear instructions on how to do so." This move prompted the reaction of the chairman of the Central Asian Bureau, Zelenskii, who, on June 23, ordered the republican Party organs to put off all measures against the Muslim "clergy" (and, one supposes, against the religious waqf they were still relying upon) until the autumn and "after an accurate preparation" had been completed. He also reminded them that local Party organs could not take any initiative of their own in this respect, and should instead obtain the endorsement of the (republican) central committee. So it is certain that the Uzbek Party organs endorsed a resolution "on the Muslim clergy," but the Central Asian Bureau itself apparently feared an acceleration in that direction, especially in the form of local "experiments." In short, throughout the summer of 1927, "the fate of religious waqf was still under consideration." Only in September 1928, would an order to confiscate religious waqf (at least in the former Fergana, Samarkand, Tashkent, and Zeravshan provinces) be issued at the republican level: but before then, as we will see below, religious waqf had already been expropriated in the Aim canton, on the basis of a very exceptional "local" decree.

At the local level, we know that the Andijan executive bureau endorsed the positions of the 13th Plenum between March and October 1927. In an undated project of resolution, it recommended the "prompt expropriation of religious waqfs" and lamented that not even all the cultural ones had been na- tionalized. However, in the same meeting at the beginning of August when it decided to send the first activists to Aim in preparation for the reform, the executive bureau of the Andijan okrkom seemed to hesitate and to backtrack: it decided to put off (vozderzhat'sia) the enactment of the Uzbek central committee's directive "on the Muslim clergy" (the one the Central Asian Bureau had approved in May). It even ordered all the local (raion) committees to refrain from taking action on this front without instructions from Andijan. Overall in Summer 1927 the Andijan okrkom sat on the fence and showed little intention of rushing into action without appropriate preparation or cover, because they were unwilling to confront a prominent Andijani Islamic leader and former head of the local mahkama-i shari'a, one Sheykh Mavlavi. However, in this the Andijani communists were ostensibly obeying Zelenskii's message to the Uzbek Party on June 23. This wait-and-see behavior is visible in the policy towards school buildings: in July 1927 the Andijan okrkom ordered the census of both new- and old-method schools and a feasibility study of their transformation into Soviet schools, as the central committee had asked.

The destruction of madrasas and the subsequent use of their building materials for new Soviet schools took place in the summer months, which raised some protests among the population and pushed the Andijan executive office of the Party to appoint an inquiring commission. On the basis of the latter's report, at the end of August the okrkom suspended the demolitions. The recycling of building materials was to be allowed on a case-by-case basis, and only after the population had filed a written request. The situation was further complicated by a sequence of earthquakes in Namangan, starting on 12 August 1927. These events received millenarian interpretations, which negatively affected the impact of Soviet anti-religious propaganda. Even Yuldash Akhunbabaev, the president of the republican central executive committee, was not able to calm the population, when he visited the district affected by the seism.

The same hesitation, not unsurprisingly, characterized the implementation in Andijan of the part of the same resolution "on the Muslim clergy" that pertained to pious endowments: through the summer of 1927, the liquidation of all waqfs (religious and residual "cultural" ones) was put off until the conclusion of the work of a local "commission on the clergy," and their management temporarily handed over to a reliable individual, one Nizambaev.

"RELIGIOUS" WAQF AND THE LAND REFORM IN AIM

Now, having examined how the destiny of waqf had evolved in the central years of the decade and what was the position of Party and Soviet organs at different levels (the Central Asian Bureau in Tashkent, the republican government in Samarkand, and the Andijan provincial committee), we need to go back to the canton of Aim and to its very peculiar situation. The Aim case is exceptional in many ways, including that of being relatively well-documented.

Provincial archives in modern Uzbekistan remain beyond the reach of most foreign scholars; besides, the "assault" (udarnyi) nature of the land reform in 1925 meant that decisions of this kind left little written trace. Instead, the fact that the land reform in Aim took place later than elsewhere means that copies of the preparatory documents and of detailed reports were sent back to the republican government.

This allows a systematic glimpse into local administrative procedures and measures, while for other localities this knowledge is largely limited to anecdotal evidence. As far as Party documents are concerned, all we have now are carbon copies of paperwork which the Uzbek Party sent to the Central Asian Bureau. Even for Aim we cannot access materials from the party cells of each rural community, or from the volost' level. And yet, the exceptional nature of the reform in Aim means that what pertained to it found its way into the documents produced by the Party at the provincial (okrug) level, and above.

The decree for the land reform in Aim is the first measure that systematically encroached on the status of religious waqf holdings. The richness of the materials available for Aim illustrates the genesis of the parts of the decree concerning the categories of people and land subject to expropriation, especially that of the articles concerning pious endowments. I have discussed the enactment of the decree and the way social categories were manipulated in the course of the reform elsewhere. The next pages will show how this shift in the regulation of the relations between the Soviet State and Islamic institutions did not take place without fight or embarrassment, first of all between Soviet and Party organs.

In particular, I demonstrate that the task of implementing directives on religious waqf expressed by the 13th Plenum of the Central Asian Bureau in May 1927 was at some point enthusiastically taken on by the Andijan Party organs, despite and against resistance from segments of the republican government in Samarkand, and even from the Central Asian Bureau. The resulting "triangle" between Samarkand (capital of the Uzbek USR), Tashkent (the Central Asian Bureau), and Andijan is suggestive of a more complex chain of command than that of "center-region-republic-province." Instead, it indicates the striking role played by the regional (i.e. Central Asian) level, and the existence of a direct connection between the Central Asian Bureau and Andijan.

The archival evidence that pertains to the drafting process of the decree includes documents in Russian: this language was used both in Samarkand and in Andijan, and it appears that only the final version of the decree was translated into Uzbek. While communists in the Aim district might have been unfamiliar with Russian, in all likelihood they did not participate in the preparation of the decree. By applying quasi-philological methods, one can count six steps in the drafting of the body of the decree, and three variants of its introduction, each of them differing from the previous one in more or less substantial details.

These variants are not classified in any particular order in the file itself (from the archive of the Administration for land settlement of the Uzbek Narkomzem), so the reconstruction of the order is mine. This section discusses first the variants in the introduction to the decree, and then moves on to consider the fight around the article about pious endowments.

The differences between the three introductions seem to have been dictated by rhetorical concerns: the first variant contained a reference to the forthcoming 10th anniversary of the October revolution and to the need to enact its slogans; the second, more pragmatic, explained that the reform in Aim was taking place to harmonize its situation with that of the rest of the okrug; the third, which would be adopted as a basis for more substantial changes in the body of the decree, was a copy-and-paste from the decree for the reform in the Zeravshan province at the end of 1926. A detail worth noting is that, in the first variant, an unknown hand had felt the need to cancel a passage mentioning "toiling land usage" (trudovoe zemlepol'zovanie), while maintaining the reference to "the destruction of the conditions of oppression of the rural poor population (kishlachnaia bednota) and of the toiling peasants by the rich, conditions which have come into existence on because of the private property on land and water." The hand that advocated such changes might have been that of someone who thought it worth insisting on the "class struggle" side of the land reform, rather than on the promise to improve the living standards of the "toiling peasantry." Finally, the first and second variants of the introduction explained the present decree as a development of the decree on the reform in Fergana two years before, while the third did not include such a reference.

This third variant of the introduction opened what I will call the first variant of the body of the decree, which was interpolated to a much greater extent than the first lines. This first variant of the body was not written from scratch, but literally resulted from the copy-and-pasting, with scissors and glue, of a printed version of the Zeravshan decree. To this printed text, an unknown hand (which I will call A) added interpolations in pencil. Some of the changes made to the Zeravshan decree were minor or obvious: for instance, the expropriation of former officials (chinovniki) of the Bukharan emirate would have made no sense in Aim, while the Zeravshan text elaborated on the land rights of eligible re-immigrants more diffusely than the Aim text, which only mentioned a very close (and probably impossible) deadline for those who wanted to return from abroad and be entitled to some land. Other changes, on the contrary, were more momentous: for instance, instead of the officials of the emirate, the Aim decree mentioned the expropriation of "those elements who exerted a particularly obnoxious influence on the population" and even their forced resettlement outside the Andijan okrug. No provision of this kind existed in the 1925 and 1926 decrees on the land reform.

The most controversial point, however, seems to have been art. 5(b) of the Zeravshan decree, which became art. 3(b) in the Aim one. This article originally stated that landless peasants and smallholders (bezzemel'nye i malozemel'nye dekhkane) should receive, among others, the land of "cultural-educational waqf, which are not in [a state of] toiling land usage" (kul'turno-prosvetitel'nykh vaku- fov, ne nakhodiashchikhsia v trudovom pol'zovanii).[75] This expression of the original Zeravshan decree was echoed in art. 2 of the instruction that went with it, which stated:

Ascribe to toiling households, within the limits of the standards for that district, all the lands that are in [a state of] toiling land usage and used to belong, at the time of the emirate, to cultural-educational **waqf,** in order to formalize finally their rights of usage and to liquidate all the exactions, which in hard times have been weighing on the shoulders of the peasantry.

While art. 5(b) (now 3(b)) was not interpolated, two different hands (A and B) changed art. 2 of the instruction twice, with the aim of merging the instruction itself into the decree for Aim. Both their modifications obeyed

34

the same rationale: to ascribe, with rights of "toiling land use" unlimited in time, not only the land of cultural-educational waqf, but also the land stock belonging to the State (GZI, gosudarstvennye zemel'nye imushchestva), to those who, until then, had tilled them as sharecroppers or on the basis of a rent contract (either paying or for free). In this way, writers A and B aimed at increasing the land stock for redistribution.

This first version (i.e. the copy-and-paste from the Zeravshan decree, but with at least two rounds of penciled handwritten changes) was replaced by a second one, written on a typewriter. One can imagine that the first and these "second" versions came from the either the Narkomzem, or from the Andijan provincial zemotdel, or from both of them at the same time. The second version (typed) maintained the same formulation of art. 5(b), but dropped from it the reference to "toiling land usage": cultural-educational waqf were to be redistributed, whether there were peasants cultivating them or not. The second version did not contain what we have referred to above as art. 2 of the Zeravshan instruction — quite likely, because at this point it had been decided not to merge the decree and the instruction for Aim.

This typed second version, though, was itself altered by two more different hands. The most controversial point was clearly the reference to the land of pious endowments. On the basis of the typed version, a firsthand (C) added in pencil that the land "of cultural-educational and religious waqf" (emphasis mine) should be expropriated and redistributed. Subsequently, another hand (D), with a pencil of a different color, struck out this reference to the religious waqfs. It is interesting to note that the same pencil used to add "religious waqf" was also used to write, at the top of this draft, "Project of the Andijan okrug." This "title" could refer to the Andijan zemotdel, or to the Andijan Party committee, or to a joint meeting of the two, or to any other local organ; moreover, it could refer either to the typed text or, more probably, to the typed text plus the first alteration (by C). What matters most, is that organs in Andijan evidently inclined towards the inclusion of religious waqf among the real estate subject to expropriation, while other political and administrative agencies (quite likely, the Narkomzem's Administration for land organization) did not feel this need. This is what we can infer from the documents of the Uzbek Administration for land organization.

However, if we look at the local Party documents available in Moscow, it becomes clear that the addendum referring to the religious waqfs came from the Andijan committee of the Party: in the meeting of its executive bureau on 1 November 1927, it proposed the introduction of such a reference, and it also suggested a set of other changes that coincided exactly with the interpolation to what we have called the "second" version (typed). It also becomes clear that, at this juncture and in Andijan, the osmosis between okrug Party organs and the zemotdel was very strong: despite the fact that he was not a member of the executive bureau, it was Mir-Isakov (the chair of the zemotdel) who presented the draft.

This interpretation is confirmed by an examination of a third version of the decree. This third version was organized in two columns: the first one presented a draft of the Andijan zemotdel, which integrated the mention of religious waqf among the "victims" of the land reform in Aim; the second, a draft by the republican people's commissariat for agriculture, which differed from the other, among other things, because it excluded religious waqf. The Nar- komzem was allegedly waiting for an overall republican policy on this matter to be adopted, and hesitated to approve the acceleration which the Andijan Party committee was trying to impose.

Despite these arguments, a further (fourth) version, titled "Decree: Project of the Narkomzem," basically coincided with the "peripheral" draft of the

Andijan zemotdel, rather than the "central" draft of the commissariat for agriculture itself. Whatever doubts the latter may have had, at some point — for reasons we will probably never know — it was forced, or convinced, to accept the nationalization and redistribution of all waqf land, whether its yield served educational institutions or mosques.

At this point, we can infer that the drafting process had definitely moved to the Samarkand republican government: arguments from Andijan had been considered, objected to, and finally, somewhat unexpectedly, integrated. Was this the end of the process? Quite the contrary. In Samarkand, it was obviously necessary to have the draft decree translated, and sent to the press. We must always remember that all those concerned (the multiple "co-authors" of the decree) were working under pressure: they engaged in a race against time to publish the decree approximately on the occasion of the 10th anniversary of the Bolshevik revolution, and to have all the operations connected to the reform finished in time not to perturb the Spring sowing campaign.

This pressure might explain why the first translation produced by the Narkomzem coincided with the third Narkomzem version (excluding religious waqfs), rather than with the subsequent fourth version (which included them). This is a sign of the considerable degree of uncertainty surrounding this issue in the central offices of the Uzbek people's commissariat for agriculture: this change was endorsed so abruptly that the translation process could simply not keep track with it, or maybe the translation was conducted on an earlier draft of the decree because only a few people were actually up-to-date with the discussions. In this translation, the mention of religious waqfs had to be included at the last minute (again, as a handwritten addendum), just before the text was sent on to the vernacular newspapers that finally published it.

The final decree was approved by the central executive committee and by the Sovnarkom of the Uzbek republic on 13 November 1927. It was identical to what we called the fourth version in the part concerning pious endowments (i.e. it included religious waqf), although it differed from it in that it excluded rain-fed land from the scope of the land reform, provided that it was not left unproductive. It would be clear to the reader how the historian who only looked at this final decree might be tempted to produce a black-and-white narrative where the Uzbek republican government is said to have unleashed the attack on religious waqf on the occasion of the land reform in Aim.

On the contrary, a close examination of the way this decree was drafted, although limited by the extant documentation, reveals a few interesting facts: first, that there existed a clear difference of views between the Andijan provincial obzem and the Uzbek republican people's commissariat for agriculture; second, that the more radical views of the former on the issue of religious waqf prevailed in an abrupt way; third, that until the very end, in the people's commissariat for agriculture, there existed considerable confusion on the line to follow, to the point of almost disseminating an incorrect Uzbek translation of the decree.

One must stress that these conflicting views existed in the people's commissariat for agriculture, which one might imagine would be closely adhering to Bolshevik ideological tropes and less scrupulous about the future of Islamic religious institutions, or about the religious sensitivity of the population, if compared to — for instance — the Narkompros.

But why were the Andijan Party organs so eager to display their will to run ahead of the Narkomzem itself and apply the reform to religious waqfs, too? It was surely not because of the very high density of religious waqf holdings in the Aim canton, or in the six rural communities concerned. It is

38

however impossible to answer this question conclusively on the basis of the available documentation. Here I will limit myself to a conjectural explanation, based upon the set of incentives that existed for the Andijan Party organs and which they were very reasonably responding to. These incentives are inferred from the issues that appeared on the agenda of the Andijan Party okrkom, of its executive bureau, and of the provincial Party committee in the crucial period in which the decree was being drafted.

In particular, the stenographic minutes of the 2nd Party conference of the Andijan okrug, which took place just on the eve of the reform, at the end of October 1927 reveals a tension (also visible elsewhere) between an Andijan group and the Party leadership in Namangan.

Before the redefinition of internal administrative units (raionirovanie), Namangan and Andijan were two separate districts (uezdy); from 1927, they were merged in the same okrug, centered in Andijan, which obviously displeased those in Namangan, whose Party organ was demoted from the status of uezd-and-city committee (ugorkom) on a par with Andijan, to that of rayon-and-city committee (raigorkom), while the Andijan one became an okrug-level organ.

This tension focused around a certain Alimov, who had tried, but failed, to secure the leadership of Namangan Party structures before the raionirovanie. According to one of his adversaries who spoke at the Andijan party conference in October 1927, Alimov had started building up his patronage networks at the time of the land-and-water reform, when he managed to be appointed as the chair of the local commission: thanks to this, he had managed to have a protege of his promoted from chair of the "collaboration cell" to secretary of the local Party cell. Alimov had managed to avoid involvement in the struggle between different Party factions and, in this way, in 1927 he still retained significant power networks locally: a

39

circumstance that allowed him, for instance, to control the appointments to the local oil plant and, allegedly, to find jobs for his supporters despite their dubious "class" background. Although the battle between Namangan and Andijan had very mundane objects (for instance, the cooperative network), the degree of engagement of one or the other center with the anti-Islamic hujum campaign was used as a weapon: the more one could claim to be active — and possibly successful — in the enactment of Party decisions against the "clergy," religious schools, and so on, the more one would secure prestige to advance on less ideological terrain.

For instance, an important step in the build-up of tensions between Namangan and Andijan just before the 2nd Party conference and the land reform in Aim had been a clash between Party activists, who were agitating in the framework of the hujum campaign, and the population of Shurkurgan. The "clergy" and the population of this locality ostensibly put up a very strong and violent opposition to the "unveiling" campaign. This should not have come as a surprise, as Shurkurgan was not new to this kind of reaction: it had been the theatre of similar clashes between Party activists and the population, led by the local "clergy," in 1925, when the former intervened in support of the squatters, soon disowned by their superiors at the republican level.

Namangan was explicitly condemned, on that occasion, for having handled the issue in a profoundly incompetent fashion, in particular by not having adequately instructed the local committee on Party policy towards the emancipation of women. This blame inevitably trickled down to the local Soviet system: the deputy chair of the Namangan district executive committee was arrested shortly after. While the Namangan gorraikom had provided guidance to Shurkurgan organs before this incident, after that the Andijan okrkom claimed such leadership for itself, for instance by excluding

Namangan from the preparations for the extraordinary renewal of the Shurkurgan rayon Soviet.

One must highlight that, at this stage, the principal actors on the political scene of the Andijan and Namangan districts, as reflected in Party documents, were without doubt local Muslims — and a Muslim was the head of the provincial branch of the People's Commissariat for Agriculture, which had typically been in the hands of European (and often, Tsarist) experts up until the 1925 land reform. While a couple of European names crop up, the horizon in which the competition between the Andijan and Namangan Party organs took place was overwhelmingly a "native" and local one — or, occasionally, one that took into account the reverberations of "factionalism" and its repression in Samarkand.

The scene we are looking at is populated by Uzbek Party members, who were worried about the local cooperative network, top jobs in oil plants, and the allocation of power positions after the raionirovanie had reshuffled the pre-existing landscape of village and district cells. Conversely, these worries translated into incentives these Party members responded to: by brushing up their ideological credentials and showing that they were "better Bolsheviks" than their neighbors, they could hope to oust their competitors. This would have secured them a better placement in the struggle for influence that followed the raionirovanie, but also the reasonable hope for some extra public spending on their district.

The presence of an exceptional situation (the "arrival" of six village communities from Kirgizia) was more than the Andijan group could hope for, and it came just at the right time. For one thing, the land reform as such represented an enormous economic opportunity for the local cooperative system, which would serve as a channel for the distribution of State credit from the Agricultural Bank (Sel'khozbank). All major organizations were involved: the local Mihnat and Omach, the district cotton co-operative, and, through its Party cell, the consumers' cooperative Uzbekberlash.[94] All this would have been the case even without the inclusion of religious waqf among the estates that were seized and redistributed — and given the skepticism with which the Narkomzem was meeting such inclusion, Andijan was taking the risk of having credit, fertilizers, and agronomic help from the latter curtailed, rather than augmented. It was not the Narkomzem that the Andijan Party elite was trying to impress, but the upper echelons of the Party — and in particular the Central Asian Bureau.

The decision to go beyond what had been, until then, the pattern of the land reform, allowed the Andijani Party elite to posit itself as an avant-garde, in striking contrast with the ineffectiveness displayed by their Namangani neighbors in the Shurkurgan events. In addition, one can hypothesize that the Central Asian Bureau could have been sensitive to the fact that, by introducing the reference to religious waqf, the Andijan okrkom was running ahead of the neighboring Kirgiz AUSR, too. According to Loring, the decree for the land reform in Osh, on the other side of the border, only targeted the holdings of "cultural" waqf. The extant documentation, however, supports the interpretation that the inclusion of religious waqf in the decree was an attempt to settle a score at the intra-republican (or even "intra-provincial"), rather than vis their Kirgiz neighbors.

That the Andijani Party leaders were responding to contingent incentives, rather than sincerely aiming at the expropriation of religious waqf landholdings, is indirectly signaled by the fact that their priority was to pass such an "advanced" decree, not to get hold of the waqf the latter mentioned. The land reform led to the confiscation of some 10,800 tanap (ca. 1,800 desiatiny) of land but, according to the summary report at the end of the reform, not a single tanap had come from the expropriation of waqf, either "religious" or "cultural." While this probably happened because these categories were conflated with others (for instance, that of "non-toiling households"), it is still interesting that this final report, addressed to the Narkomzem, did not even mention the expropriation of waqf. On the contrary, at the same time the executive bureau of the Andijan okrkom was very anxious about the press coverage of the reform, to the point of protesting with the editors of Yangi Farghona. It was important to give the impression that Andijan was energetically and quickly embracing the "hard line" towards Islamic religious institutions: in a short-term horizon at least, local Party elites were acting as if they believed that this was enough to gain political credit with the upper Party echelons.

Such an achievement would be considered all the greater, as the six rural communities of Aim were still allegedly untouched by sovietization. Not only could a speaker, Ashurov, tell the other participants at a Party conference that in Aim one hundred mosques had been destroyed for a population of one thousand inhabitants (which was an exaggeration, but a meaningful one)—he could also contrast these results, and those that the reform would bring about, with a situation which he portrayed as initially desperate. There were already seventeen people currently under trial.

The land reform will take place, [but] the Soviet **apparat** there is so contaminated **(zasoren)** that it is simply impossible, and as a result of such contamination **(zasorennost')** even such a thing can happen: [that] the chair of the village Soviet **(sel'sovet)** is such a [kind of] person, who for five years studied in a **madrasa,** and for twelve years, under the old regime, used to be a village elder **(starshina; i.e. aksakai).** For five years he served at the mosque **(scil.** as **imam)** and all his relatives are religious staff **(sviashchenniki),** sacred people **(sviatye liudy).** He owned 36 **tanaps** of land—and this is the chair of the village Soviet! When one looks at him, one

43

immediately sees a Tsarist village elder.

Depicting a nightmarish—in the Bolshevik mind-set—situation to exalt subsequent meagre results was clearly a consolidated argumentative strategy, which in the case of the land reform in Aim could be used over and over again: at the same conference, one Shamansurov reminded the audience that in Aim "if someone has a horse and some land, that someone is elected as chair of the executive committee—and there is not a chair, but [just] an **aksakal,"** such as the one who had allegedly tried to hide 130 **tanaps** (more than 20 desiatiny). To have decided to attack religious **waqf** for the first time in such an unfavorable context was an act of courage that, one hoped, would sooner or later bear fruit.

CONCLUSION: THE EXPERIMENT SPILLS OVER

Islam has been shaped as a system of indispensable values for thousands of years in the history of peoples, especially in the peoples of our region, in the vast territories of the earth. As President Mirziyoyev said, "We believe that the main task of the entire world community is to convey the essence of the true humanitarian essence of the Islamic religion (Novak & Schwabe, 2009; Razakov Sh & Shakhgunova, 2001).

We value our sacred religion as an expression of our perpetual values. The religion of Islam encourages us to live in goodness and peace and preserve original human qualities. "However, at the beginning of the Russian colonial period, during the Soviet totalitarian system, at the time of the Soviet colonialism and the values associated with it, artificially destroyed, or even some of the values were destroyed. One of such values is the Founding Institute, which was completed in 1928 in Uzbekistan. But it should be studied and studied as an integral part of our historical and cultural heritage and our past. Because statehood, education, social protection, prosperity, agriculture and the economic system were directly linked to the foundation property of the past.

In historic sources and historical documents, we find documents and information about foundations and foundations. As in the case of the falsification of the true history during the Soviet era and the devastation of the millennial traditions of our people, the concept of the founda- tion was very limited and unambiguous, and the concept of the foundation was introduced only in relation to the place of mosque and madrasahs. It is sad to say that even a great number of historian scholars only define the definition and the concept above. In fact, the concept of the foundation is a concept, value, or socio-spiritual institution that plays a very important role in our religious, spiritual and socio-economic life that needs to be interpreted

45

in a broader sense(Blank, 2013; Connell, 2006; psychologica & 1970, n.d.).

This complex entanglement of local motivations and opportunities, against the background of a shifting (but still somewhat hesitant) political attitude towards the Islamic "clergy" of Central Asia, resulted in the confiscation of religious waqf in six rural communities of the Aim canton of the Andijan province about one year earlier than in the rest of Fergana—and, indeed, in the rest of the Uzbek republic. In other words, the very local decree that resulted from the process outlined above was the first normative measure that encroached on the very existence of the pious endowments of mosques, shrines, and khanaqas, if one excludes local "administrative" decisions taken in the early years of Soviet rule and then rejected by the Soviet official line. This shift represented an obvious escalation in the gradual tightening of the relations between Soviet rule in Central Asia and local Islamic institutions—and Islamic practice itself. Repairs, building works, and the employment of community leaders could not be funded by means of waqf revenues any more.

And yet, such a major shift occurred as a result of pressures from local Soviet and, above all, Party organs, which ran ahead of Samarkand on the terrain of anti-religious policy, and did so in order to position themselves as "better," more orthodox, and more militant Bolsheviks than their peers in other locali- ties—above all, relative to their neighbors in Namangan. It is true that general directives on religious schools and waqfs had come from the Central Asian Bureau of the all-Union Party: in this, Andijan was not acting without external inspiration. Yet, it was not granted that the Bureau's directives should be implemented immediately, without adaptations. In this respect, it is significant that it was the local level that first appropriated them, while Samarkand was lagging behind, but was finally forced to yield.

The Andijan party committee itself had oscillated between a radical line, favorable to the swift implementation of the Central Asian Bureau's directives on religious schools and waqfs, and a more prudent attitude, which persuaded it, in September 1927, to defer the application of the Uzbek Party directive "on the Muslim clergy" to the moment when a specific local instruction would become available. In the case of the reform in Aim, it was the first line that pre- vailed – possibly because in this case the Andijan Party authorities wanted to "show off" to their competitors in Namangan. But elsewhere, this was not the case: even the executive bureau of the Andijan okrkom would endorse a clear, comprehensive line on the waqf issue only in March 1928, when it excluded the possibility that any sort of waqf land should be rented out, and ruled that it should be redistributed, for free, to landless and smallholding peasants. (This was what had happened in Aim months before.) Until then, waqf estates had remained under the (direct or indirect, and surely problematic) control of the Narkompros: after March 1928, on the contrary, the Narkompros and its local agencies only captured the (relatively) small income generated by waqfs on goods other than land, in particular bazaar stalls.

Inevitably, this wholesale attack on waqf revenues eroded the margins of maneuver of the GVU and its branches, leading to the curtailment of religious schools. All this was paralleled by the definitive crisis of the mahkama-i shari'a, which ended up liquidating themselves in an array of cities by June 1928. It was only at the beginning of August 1928, though, that a resolution of the central bureau of the Uzbek communist Party ordered that the Narkomzem should receive all religious waqf, including orchards and vineyards, and that such a transfer should be completed in two months. As had happened on the occasion of the land reform in the "core provinces" and in the Zeravshan oblast', this move meant the inclusion of this land in the stock (fond) available for redistribution. In homage to the new Zeitgeist, which claimed the superiority of collective farms on individual sustainable smallholdings, the land from liquidated waqf could be ascribed to the new kolkhozy. Needless to say, once again the Andijan okrkom managed to carve out a space for "acceleration" in the process of wholesale land organization and collectivization, by insisting on the constitution of an "experimental district" in Assaka (now Asaka), located at 16 km to the south-west of Andijan, on the main road between the latter and Margelan.

In the absence of a detailed prosopography of all those involved, it would be premature (but surely tempting) to hypothesize the existence of an Andijan power clique, which consistently tried to put itself forward as a model of Bolshevik activism, especially as far as the transformation of agrarian relations was concerned. Yet, it seems clear that, in the mid-1920s, the local political context was ripe for acceleration and experimental initiatives. The revision of the border in the Aim district provided an ideal opportunity to propose and enact, on a small scale, something for which the rest of the Uzbek USR was not quite ready, according to the Party organs and the government in Samarkand—and even according to the Central Asian Bureau in Tashkent. In this, a modification of the inter-republican border, though occurring three years after the delimitation proper, had momentous consequences both for provincial political actors and for the rural dwellers that were most directly concerned by the land reform. Even more importantly, when combined with the ambitions of local politicians, the amendment of the border in Aim constituted the background for a radical shift in the way the Soviet State in Uzbekistan dealt with the residual category of pious endowments that so far had managed to survive.

Blanket narratives that attempt to summarise the phases of such a dramatic change across the Uzbek republic as a whole, or even across the different Central Asian republics, have failed to pin down both the local

48

reactions to the 1924 delimitation process, and the zigzags that preceded the attack on the most problematic of all categories of waqf. While the post-Soviet community of historians often regards such a practice as mere kraevedenie, delving into the local and the detail in a systematic, rather than anecdotal, way is an essential exercise to reconstruct chains of command and forms of political culture that ultimately affected the republic (if not the region) as a whole. Local examples are not just illustrations that add texture to the historical narrative: they are the very bricks from which a more thorough and rigorous reconstruction of the events can emerge. While the word "Vaqf" has been exaggerated today, most of the cultural heritage left by our ancestors survived so far. There is almost no idea of the foundation of the foundation. However, as we have stated above, it is extremely important to restore this value based on the fact that only the foundation is a publicly understood value, without the understanding of mosques and madrasahs. In fact, as a foundation work, it is possible to deliver drinking water to the population on the basis of new technologies instead of solving water problems by digging a well. The need for water is still very important today. An example of this is the fact that Muynak district is being built. The organization of gas pipelines, bridges, roads, gardens, private schools, as well as private hospitals, libraries and others is of paramount importance today. Today, if good deeds, based on the Islamic religion, can be introduced into the social life of our people, the entrepreneurial and entrepreneurial citizens who have the financial ability to direct their resources to good deeds, the social situation in our country will grow and the welfare of our people will grow. The implementation of the development strategy for socio-economic and cultural development of the country for 2017-2021 will be ensured.

REFERENCES

[1]. Blank, S. (2013). Why the Lean Start Up Changes Everything. Harvard Business Review, 91(5), 64. https://doi.org/10.1109/Agile.2012.18

[2]. Connell, J. (2006). Medical tourism: Sea, sun, sand and surgery. Tourism Management, 27(6), 1093–1100. https:doi.org.

[3]. Fathi, H. (2006). Gender, Islam, and social change in Uzbekistan. Central Asian Survey, 25(3), 303–317. https://doi.org/10.1080/02634930601022575

[4]. Haq, F., & Yin Wong, H. (2010). Is spiritual tourism a new strategy for marketing Islam? Journal of Islamic Marketing, 1(2), 136–148. https://doi.org/10.1108/17590831011055879

[5]. Karagiannis, E. (2006). Political Islam in Uzbekistan: Hizb ut-Tahrir al-Islami. Europe - Asia Studies, 58(2), 261–280. https://doi.org/10.1080.

[6]. Mohamed, B., Som, A. P. M., Jusoh, J., & Kong, Y. W. (2006). Island Tourism in Malaysia. In 12th Asia Pacific Tourism Association & 4th Asia Pacific CHRIE Joint Conference (pp. 1212–1219).

[7]. Newswire, P. (2012). Asia Medical Tourism Analysis and Forecast to 2015 . PR Newswire US. 10/22/2012. Document Type:ArticleGeographic Terms:New YorkAbstract:NEW YORK, 2015, 01015266/Asia-<strong xmlns:translation="urn:EBSCO.

[8]. Razakov Sh, A., & Shakhgunova, Gs. (2001). [Current malaria situation in the Republic of Uzbekistan]. Med Parazitol (Mosk), (1), 39–41. Retrieved from http:// www.ncbi.nlm.nih. gov/pubmed/11548313

[9]. Spechler, D. R., & Spechler, M. C. (2009). Uzbekistan among the great powers. Communist and Post-Communist Studies, 42(3), 353–373. https://doi.org/10.1016/ j.postcomstud. 2009.07.006

[10]. Keller, To Moscow, Not Mecca, p. 153 (on the basis of: Ispolbiuro TsK KPUz, protokol No. 51, 1.8.1928, RGASPI, f. 62, op.

[11]. Ispolbiuro Andijan OK KP(b)Uz, protokol N 15 (extraordinary meeting), 19.3.1928, RGASPI, f. 17, op. 16, d. 159, ll. 133-136, here l. 135; cf. Nizambaev's speech at the 3rd Plenum Andijan OK KP(b)Uz, 23-25.5.1928, ibid., ll. 1-100.

[12]. Nizambaev's speech at the 3rd Plenum Andijan OK KP(b)Uz, 23-25.5.1928, ibid., ll. 1-100.

[13]. Benjamin H. Loring, "Rural Dynamics and Peasant Resistance in Southern Kyrgyzstan, 1929-1930," Cahiers du Monde Russe 49:1 (2008), pp. 183-210, here p. 190 (source unclear). In his dissertation Loring excludes the confiscation of "religious" waqfbecause he assumes that the 1927 land reform decree for the southern Kirgiz AUSR was identical to the 1925 Uzbek one: idem, Building Socialism in Kyrgyzstan: Nation-making, Rural Development, and Social Change, 1921-1932 (PhD diss., Brandeis University, 2008),

[14]. Andijan Ispolbiuro okrugkom PK(b)Uz, Protokol N 3, 6.12.1927, RGASPI, f. 62, op. 27, d. 156.

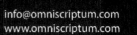

Printed in Great Britain
by Amazon